Guided Reading Notes

Brown Band
Oxford Level 11

Strong Defences

Contents

OXFORD
UNIVERSITY PRESS

Introduction

Why is guided reading important?

Guided reading plays an important role in your whole-school provision for reading, providing opportunities for children to progress and develop the key competencies they need to become confident and skilled independent readers. Working with small groups of children, with texts closely matched to the readers' needs, guided reading is the perfect vehicle for delivering focused teaching from Reception/P1 right through to Year 6/P7. The teacher-pupil interaction also provides a valuable assessment opportunity, helping you identify exactly what each child can and can't do. Through guided reading children also encounter a world of exciting, whole books – building a community of readers who read for pleasure.

About *Project X Origins*

Project X Origins is a comprehensive, whole-school guided reading programme designed to help you teach the wide range of skills essential to ensure children progress as readers and to help nurture a love of reading.

Ensuring the key skills are covered

Project X Origins incorporates all of the key skills children need to develop to become successful and enthusiastic readers:

- **Word reading:** phonically regular and common exception words are introduced systematically in the early levels with phonic opportunities provided throughout the notes. As children progress, they are encouraged to use their decoding skills whenever they encounter new or unfamiliar words, and also to recognize how this impacts on different spelling rules.

- **Comprehension:** understanding what has been read is central to being an effective and engaged reader but comprehension is not something that comes automatically so specific strategies have been built into the notes to ensure children develop comprehension skills they can use over a range of texts:
  - Previewing
  - Predicting
  - Activating and building prior knowledge
  - Questioning
  - Recalling
  - Visualizing and other sensory responses
  - Deducting, inferring and drawing conclusions
  - Determining importance
  - Synthesizing
  - Empathizing
  - Summarizing
  - Personal response, including adopting a critical response
- **Reading fluency:** fluency occurs as children develop automatic word recognition, reading with pace and expression. Strategies to help achieve this, including meaningful opportunities for oral reading, re-reading and re-listening are provided throughout.
- **Vocabulary:** introducing new vocabulary within a meaningful context is an important element in extending children's vocabulary range, developing their reading fluency and comprehension. Each thematic cluster provides opportunities for revisiting and reinforcing vocabulary over a range of books and contexts.
- **Grammar, punctuation and spelling:** learning about language in the context of a text, rather than through a series of discrete exercises, can help make grammar, punctuation and spelling relevant and helps children make the link between grammar, punctuation and clarity of meaning, thus supporting their development as writers. Opportunities to support an in-depth look at language are provided for every book from Year 1/P2 to Year 6/P7.
- **Spoken language:** talk is crucial to learning and developing their comprehension so children are given plenty of opportunities to: discuss and debate their ideas with others; justify their opinions; ask and answer questions; explore and hypothesise; summarise, describe and explain; and listen and respond to the ideas of others.

Assessment and progression in reading

Project X Origins includes a rigorous assessment spine drawn from the *Oxford Ros Wilson Reading Criterion Scale* to ensure that you know exactly what each child can do and what they need to focus on next in order to make progress. This assessment framework, combined with the careful levelling of the Oxford Levels, will help you select the right book with the right level of challenge for each of your guided reading groups and to assess, track and monitor each child's progress.

Step 1

On a termly basis, use the *Reading Criterion Scale* (which can be found in the relevant *Project X Origins Teaching Handbook*) to assess each child's reading. The scale will tell you the Oxford Level a child is comfortable reading at, and the areas a child needs to develop. You can also use this assessment to form your guided reading groups.

Step 2

Plan your guided reading sessions by selecting books at the appropriate Oxford Level that focus on the relevant learning needs of the group. You will find charts showing the learning objectives and assessment points for every *Project X Origins* book in the relevant *Project X Origins Teaching Handbook*. Depending on your assessment, you might choose a book at the level the children are comfortable at or one from the next level up, to offer some stretch.

Step 3

Use the assessment points within the Guided Reading Notes to support on-going assessment of children's reading progress. The Progress Tracking Charts in the relevant *Project X Origins Teaching Handbook* can be used to record this if you wish. Regularly re-assess each child's progress combining your on-going informal assessments and the termly assessment using the *Reading Criterion Scale*. Use this information to re-organize guided reading groups and teaching plans in response to children's varying degrees of progress.

Getting started: using the Guided Reading Notes

At a glance

Project X Origins Guided Reading Notes offer detailed guidance to help deliver effective and engaging guided reading sessions, and are designed to be used flexibly to ensure you get the most out of each book. For notes containing multiple sessions, you may choose to focus on each of these sessions or focus on one session and have the children read the rest of the book independently.

Curricula correlation and assessment

At the beginning of every set of notes there are correlation charts for all UK curricula, ensuring that across the clusters the main curricula objectives are covered. In addition, an overview of assessment points for each book is provided – these points are also signposted throughout the notes.

Key information

Before the first session, an overview of the book and the resources you will need (such as additional photocopy masters) is provided.

Teaching sequence

Each guided reading session follows the same teaching sequence:

- **Before reading**: children explore the context of each book to support their understanding and help them engage with the text. They are encouraged to discuss, recall, respond, predict and speculate about the book. Opportunities to focus on word reading and/or vocabulary are also introduced at this point.
- **During reading**: children are given a section of the book to read with specific questions in mind.
- **After reading**: children reflect on and discuss what they have read. They are encouraged to delve deeper, exploring their understanding of the text, developing their vocabulary, grammar, punctuation, spelling and fluency where appropriate.
- **Follow-up**: opportunities for children to extend their learning outside the session are provided, including writing and cross-curricular activities.

Throughout the sessions, the key strategies that children are developing are clearly identified.

The X-bots are Coming …

BY ANTHONY McGOWAN

Curricula correlation

English National Curriculum

Spoken language	Articulate and justify answers, arguments and opinions
Word reading	Apply knowledge of root words and suffixes (etymology and morphology) to understand the meaning of new words they meet
Comprehension	Infer characters' feelings, thoughts and motives from their actions and justify inferences with detailed evidence
	Discuss words and phrases that capture the reader's interest and imagination

Developing grammar, punctuation, vocabulary and spelling

Grammar and Punctuation	Introduction to inverted commas to punctuate direct speech	"Quiet, you fools," screamed Dr X.
	Use of *so* to emphasize a quality, feeling, or amount	so clever, so funny, not so easy
Vocabulary and Spelling	Challenge and context words	army, captured, castle, moat, defences, catapult, camouflaged, defend, attack, corridor, machinery, assigned, wading, sensible, assembled

Reading assessment points

Word reading	Can the children read independently using a range of strategies appropriately, including decoding, to establish meaning?
Comprehension	Can the children explain how and why main characters act in a story, using evidence from the text?
	Can the children explore potential meanings of ambitious vocabulary read in context, using knowledge of etymology (*the word origin*), morphology (*the form and structure of a word, i.e. the 'root' word plus prefix and/or suffix*), or the context of the word?
	Can the children identify where language is used to create mood, build tension or paint a picture?
	Can the children make plausible predictions based on knowledge from/of the text and wider connections?

Scottish Curriculum for Excellence

Listening and talking objectives	I can select ideas and relevant information, organize these in a logical sequence and use words which will be interesting and/or useful for others LIT 1-06a
Reading objectives	I can share my thoughts about the structure, characters and/or setting, recognize the writer's message and relate it to my own experiences and comment on the effective choice of words and other features ENG 1-19a
	I can use my knowledge of sight vocabulary, phonics, context clues, punctuation and grammar to read with understanding and expression ENG 1-12a

Welsh National Literacy Framework

Oracy	Explain information and ideas using relevant vocabulary (Speaking)
Reading	Use a range of strategies to make meaning from words and sentences, including knowledge of phonics, word roots, word families, syntax, text organisation and prior knowledge of context (Reading strategies)
	Deduce ideas and information by linking explicit statements, *e.g. cause and effect* (Comprehension)

Northern Ireland Curriculum

Talking and Listening	Listen to, interpret and retell, with some supporting detail, a range of oral and written texts
	Express thoughts, feelings and opinions in response to personal experiences, imaginary situations, literature, media and curricular topics and activities
Reading	Use a range of comprehension skills, both oral and written, to interpret and discuss texts

Session 1 (Chapters 1–3)

About this book

As Dr X has discovered the micro-friends' hideout in the old tree stump, the children move to Tiger's castle on the island of the park pond. They set up various traps to defend themselves against attack from the X-bots.

You will need

- *Den locations* Photocopy Master, *Teaching Handbook* for Year 3/P4
- *Character profile* Photocopy Master, *Teaching Handbook* for Year 3/P4
- *Castle for sale* Photocopy Master, *Teaching Handbook* for Year 3/P4

Before reading

- Look at the cover and ask the children to recall the X-bots in other stories. Do they notice anything new or different about the X-bot on the front cover? **(activating prior knowledge)**
- Show the cover of the second book (*Attack of the X-bots!*) and ask them how they think the two books might link together. **(predicting)**

Assessment point

Can the children make plausible predictions based on knowledge from/of the text and wider connections?

- Help the children decode some of the context vocabulary related to attacking and defending and use syntax and context to work out their meaning, e.g. *moat* (p.18), *defences* (p.34), *attack* (p.35), *capture* (p.37). Start creating a list of words for a word wall. **(supporting decoding, introducing new vocabulary)**

During reading

- Ask the children to read, from the beginning of the book to the end of Chapter 3.
- As they read, ask them to think about how the author shows the different emotions the friends are feeling. Ask them to jot down any vocabulary related to how they feel or act.
- If you have not already done so, ask the children what to do if they encounter a difficult word, modelling with an example from the book if necessary.

Assessment point

Can the children read independently using a range of strategies appropriately, including decoding, to establish meaning?

After reading

Returning to the text

- Ask the children to describe the friends' different reactions to the need to move their secret base. What vocabulary helps us to understand these reactions? **(recall)**
- Can the children explain why Dr X was giving Plug and Socket new roles? How did Plug and Socket feel about this? **(deducing, inferring, drawing conclusions)**
- Ask the children to identify the weakness in the plan to put the den up the tree. How did Max show leadership skills? **(determining importance)**
- Why did Max ask if everyone could swim *before* he suggested the island? What does that tell you about Max? **(deducing, inferring)**

Developing comprehension

- Ask the children to use the *Character profiles* Photocopy Master for any/all of the characters if they think they have identified new information about that character. Remind them that they must be able to quote evidence from the text. **(deducing, inferring, synthesizing)**
- Ask the children to list the pros and cons for each of the secret bases, using the *Den locations* Photocopy Master. **(deducing, inferring, drawing conclusions)**

Assessment point

Can the children explain how and why main characters act in a story, using evidence from the text?

Developing grammar, punctuation and spelling

- Draw attention to the use of inverted commas. Explain they can be used to indicate direct speech e.g. "Quiet, you fools," screamed Dr X (p.8).
- Look at the rapid exchange on pages 8 and 9 and discuss how the punctuation makes the meaning clear. How do we know who has said what? Draw attention to the use of different verbs to show how someone is speaking.

Session 2 (Chapters 4–6)

Before reading

- Ask the children to recap on the story so far. What do they think will happen in the middle of the story? **(activating prior knowledge, predicting)**
- Point out the unusual spelling of the plural word *larvae* (p.23) and ask the children to guess what the singular form is. Discuss other similar words that the children might know, e.g. *antenna/antennae*. **(supporting word recognition)**
- You may also wish to practise decoding some of the challenge and context words. **(introducing new vocabulary)**

Assessment point
Can the children explore potential meanings of ambitious vocabulary read in context, using knowledge of etymology (*the word origin*), morphology (*the form and structure of a word, i.e. the 'root' word plus prefix and/or suffix*), or the context of the word?

During reading

- Ask the children to read Chapters 4–6.
- As they read, ask them to think about how the characters, including Dr X, Plug and Socket, are thinking and feeling.
- Ask the children to look out for the use of *so* in the story.

After reading

Returning to the text

Ask the children:

- Why was the island a good base?
- What do we learn about Tiger's character from his actions in Chapter 4?
- How does the author build tension at the end of Chapter 6? **(deducing, inferring, drawing conclusions)**

Developing comprehension

- Ask the children to freeze frame the moment on page 30 when Dr X discovers the children have moved their base.

Developing grammar, punctuation and spelling

- Turn to page 23 and ask the children to look at the use of *so* in the last sentence. Explain that it is a conjunction in the sentence, connecting the last sentence with Ant's statement about the pike.
- Ask the children to find other examples of *so* in the text. How are they similar to or different from the first example? Explain that *so* can also be an adverb which emphasizes an adjective, e.g. *not so easy* (p.24), *so clever, so funny* (p.30). Can they find any more examples? How else could they say the same thing? (*so funny – hilarious*)

Session 3 (Chapters 7–9)

Before reading

- Ask the children to recap on the story so far. Reminding them that there is a sequel story (*Attack of the X-bots!*), how do they think this story will end? **(activating prior knowledge, predicting)**
- Look at the word *catapult* on page 38 and ask the children what this word means.

During reading

- Ask the children to read Chapters 7–9.
- As they read, ask them to think about how the author creates tension in these chapters.

After reading

Returning to the text

- Ask the children to briefly describe the different traps that the micro-friends devise. **(recall)**
- Ask why the micro-friends are feeling happy at the start of Chapter 9, then track how their emotions change during the chapter. (Firstly, they feel happy, become concerned, triumphant, very afraid, then finally, feel brave). Can the children spot the vocabulary, speech and actions that help them to identify these changing emotions? Which emotions do they infer? (e.g. The friend's triumph when they hit an X-bot.) **(deducing, inferring, drawing conclusions)**

- Ask the children to identify the cliffhanger at the end of the story. How does this create tension? How does it make the reader feel? **(personal response)**

Assessment point

Can the children identify where language is used to create mood, build tension or paint a picture?

Developing fluency

- Invite the children to enact some of the scenes at the NASTI headquarters, in particular Dr X's speech to the robots. Then ask them to reread these chapters aloud using as much expression as possible. **(performance)**

Follow-up

Writing activities

- Write an estate agent's blurb for the castle on the island, using the *Castle for sale* Photocopy Master. **(short writing task)**
- Write a longer speech for Dr X to deliver to the X-bots in which he tells them more about why he needs the watches, as well as praising their design, intelligence, strength, etc. **(longer writing task)**

Other possible literacy activities

- Children could perform or record for other members of the group their Dr X speech (see Writing activities).
- Children enact some of the scenes that contain direct speech, making sure that they use the punctuation and verbs to help them interpret the way that each part should be spoken. **(spoken language)**

Cross-curricular activities

- Produce a design brief for the X-bot Mark 3. **(DT)**
- Use Ant's description of pond life as the stimulus for furtherresearch on one of the creatures and their defence/attack mechanisms. **(Science)**
- Use musical instruments to create marching music for the 'March of the X-bots'. **(Music)**
- Design a film poster for the film 'The X-bots are Coming'. **(Art and Design)**

Attack of the X-bots!

BY ANTHONY McGOWAN

Curricula correlation

English National Curriculum

Spoken language	Give well-structured descriptions and explanations
Word reading	Apply knowledge of root words and suffixes (etymology and morphology) to understand the meaning of new words they meet
	Predicting what might happen from details stated and implied
Comprehension	Infer characters' feelings, thoughts and motives from their actions and justify inferences with detailed evidence
	Identify how language, structure, and presentation contribute to meaning

Developing grammar, punctuation, vocabulary and spelling

Grammar and Punctuation	Expressing time using adverbs	before, after, soon
	Use of the suffixes *-er* and *-est* in adjectives	stronger, meaner, faster, lower, earlier bravest, cleverest, best
Vocabulary and Spelling	Add the suffixes *-er* and *-est* to adjectives	stronger, meaner, faster, lower, earlier bravest, cleverest, best
	Challenge and context words	army, fight, escape, defences, scared, marched, conquer, catapult, castle, destroyed, retreat, trap, march, drawbridge, tower, circuits, magnet, magnetism, propeller, scientific, amphibious, diversion, ammunition

Reading assessment points

Word reading	Can the children read independently using a range of strategies appropriately, including decoding, to establish meaning?
Comprehension	Can the children summarise and explain the main points in a text, referring back to the text to support this?
	Can the children discuss how characters are built from small details?
	Can the children make plausible predictions based on knowledge from/of the text and wider connections?
	Can the children explain how and why main characters act in a story, using evidence from the text?

Scottish Curriculum for Excellence

Listening and talking objectives	I can select ideas and relevant information, organize these in a logical sequence and use words which will be interesting and/or useful for others LIT 1-06a
Reading objectives	I can share my thoughts about the structure, characters and/or setting, recognise the writer's message and relate it to my own experiences and comment on the effective choice of words and other features ENG 1-19a
	I am learning to select and use strategies and resources before I read, and as I read, to help make the meaning of texts clear LIT 1-13a
	I can comment on the effective choice of words and other features ENG 1-19a

Welsh National Literacy Framework

Oracy	Organise what they say so that listeners can understand, *e.g. emphasising key points, sequencing an explanation* (Speaking)
Reading	Use a range of strategies to make meaning from words and sentences, including knowledge of phonics, word roots, word families, syntax, text organisation and prior knowledge of context (Reading strategies)
	Deduce ideas and information by linking explicit statements, *e.g. cause and effect* (Comprehension)

Northern Ireland Curriculum

Talking and Listening	Express thoughts, feelings and opinions in response to personal experiences, imaginary situations, literature, media and curricular topics and activities
Reading	Express opinions and give reasons based on what they have read
	Use a range of strategies to identify unfamiliar words

Session 1 (Chapters 1–4)

About this book

This sequel to *The X-bots are Coming* ... describes how the micro-friends defend their castle from the X-bots' attack, using various strategies and traps: creating a diversion to lead them towards the pike; short-circuiting them by catapulting water balloons; trapping them with sticky bubblegum; disrupting their circuits using the magnet. Finally, Cat uses bread to entice the ducks to trample the X-bots!

You will need

- *Character profile* Photocopy Master, *Teaching Handbook* for Year 3/P4
- *Problems and outcomes* Photocopy Master, *Teaching Handbook* for Year 3/P4

Before reading

- Read pages 2 and 3 together and recap the details of the traps the micro-friends have prepared for the X-bots.
- Discuss what else will offer the children protection from attack (e.g. water, walls). **(activating prior knowledge, predicting)**
- Help the children decode some of the context vocabulary related to attacking and defending and use syntax and context to work out their meaning, e.g. *diversion* (p.11), *conquer* (p.13). Start or continue creating a list of words for a word wall. **(introduce new vocabulary)**

During reading

- Ask the children to read Chapters 1–4.
- As they read, ask them to think about the changing emotions the friends and Dr X are feeling as the attack occurs.
- If you have not already done so, ask the children what to do if they encounter a difficult word, modelling with an example from the book if necessary. Remind them of the more challenging vocabulary which you looked at before reading the book. «
- Ask the children to look for words that use the suffixes *-er* and *-est* as they read through.

Assessment point

Can the children read independently using a range of strategies appropriately, including decoding, to establish meaning?

After reading

Returning to the text

- Ask the children why the friends decided they must fight the X-bots.
- Ask the children to describe, in sequence, the first two attacks from the X-bots by water and by air, and the defences that were used by the friends. **(recall)**

Assessment point
Can the children summarise and explain the main points in a text, referring back to the text to support this?

Developing comprehension

- Talk about the different responses of each character to the X-bots' first transformation (pages 8–9). Does this add to or confirm what they already know about each child's character? Children could add to the *Character profile* Photocopy Masters for any/all of the characters. **(deducing, inferring, drawing conclusions)**
- Complete the *Problems and outcomes* Photocopy Master to show how the problems encountered in the book were overcome by the children. This can be continued after each session and will provide a prompt sheet or talking frame for children to give a sequenced, oral account of the story. **(determining importance)**

Developing grammar, punctuation and spelling

- Look at the words the children found that contain the suffix *-er*, e.g. *meaner* (p.7), *faster* (p.14). Remind children that these adjectives are called comparatives (they compare two things).
- Discuss how to make the superlative form by adding the suffix *-est* to the word. What words did they find with this ending? Explain the these adjectives are used when more than two things are being compared.
- Explain that there are exceptions to these spelling rules when the last letter of the word should be doubled, e.g. *sad - sadder - saddest, hot - hotter - hottest*. Can they think of any more? Explain that some adjectives don't follow this rule, e.g. *good - better - best*.

Session 2 (Chapters 5 and 6)

Before reading

- Recap the story so far. Encourage the children to predict what will happen next, reminding them of the traps that the friends developed beforehand. **(activating prior knowledge, predicting)**
- Continue or start to create a word wall relating to defending and attacking using words from these chapters. **(introducing new vocabulary)**

During reading

- Ask the children to read Chapters 5 and 6.
- As they read, ask them to think about the author's choice of vocabulary to show the humour in Plug and Socket.

After reading

Returning to the text

Ask the children:

- Why is the X-bot called *the X-bot mole* on page 25?
- What is it that Ant notices when Max first uses the magnet on the X-bot? (p.32) Why is this important later in the chapter?
- What do Max's actions in Chapter 6 tell us about his character? What evidence can you find to back up your views?
- As well as 'nincompoops' (p.29), what words and actions are used to show that Plug and Socket are not very clever? **(deducing, inferring, drawing conclusions)**

Assessment point

Can the children discuss how characters are built from small details?

Developing comprehension

- Start or continue to fill in the *Problems and outcomes* Photocopy Master to show how the problems encountered in the book were overcome by the friends. **(determining importance)**

Session 3 (Chapters 7–9)

Before reading

- Ask the children, in turn, to relay the events of the story so far. **(activating prior knowledge)**
- Read page 38 together. Can the children guess where Cat is going and why? **(predicting)**
- Continue your word wall relating to defending and attacking using words from these chapters.

Assessment point
Can the children make plausible predictions based on knowledge from/of the text and wider connections?

During reading

- Ask the children to read Chapters 7–9.
- As they read, ask them to think about how the characters' words and actions reveal their personalities.
- Ask them to think about how time passes during the story and to note the words the author uses to show this.

After reading

Return to the text

Ask the children:

- What do Ant and Tiger think Cat is doing when she leaves the castle? Do you agree or disagree with the way they reacted to her leaving? What are your reasons/evidence?
- Why does Max jump down from his safe refuge in the tree? What does this tell you about Max's character?
- Do Dr X and Plug and Socket have the same feelings about the failed attack?
- Why do they think the author ends the story with the final sentence? **(deducing, inferring, drawing conclusions)**

Developing comprehension

- Ask the children to fill in their *Character profile* Photocopy Master, adding evidence that shows each character's personality. **(drawing conclusions)**
- Ask the children to complete their *Problems and outcomes* Photocopy Master to use later as a prompt sheet (see Other literacy activities). **(determining importance)**

Assessment point
Can the children explain how and why main characters act in a story, using evidence from the text?

Developing grammar, punctuation and spelling

- Ask the children to identify words used to show that time has passed in the story, e.g. *before* (p.32), *after* (p.35), *soon* (p. 35).
- Explain that many of these words are adverbs, e.g. *soon*. They tell the reader how something has happened, in this case when things happened.
- Ask the children what the purpose of the word *meanwhile* is on page 37? What does this adverb tell the reader? Why is it important to know that some parts of the story are happening at the same time?

Follow-up

Writing activities

- Write an advertisement or sales blurb for the X-bot Mark 3. **(short writing task)**
- Write a newspaper report of the battle with a suitable headline. **(longer writing task)**
- Turn the scenes in NASTI headquarters into a play script. **(longer writing task)**

Other literacy activities

- Invite the children to give an oral re-telling of the story. **(spoken language, performance)**
- Ask the children to use the comparative and superlative adjectives they collected to describe a character to their partner. Can they guess who is being described? **(spoken language)**

Cross-curricular activities

- Annotate the X-bot design sheet started in *The X-bots are Coming ...* with the new features now revealed. **(DT)**
- Experiment with magnets and a selection of materials to discover which are magnetic and which cannot be magnetized. **(Science)**
- Use musical instruments to create background music for one of the chapters in the book. **(Music)**
- Devise an 'X-bot attack' board game which involves throwing dice and counting round a board. **(Maths, DT)**

Lone Wolf

BY SUSAN GATES

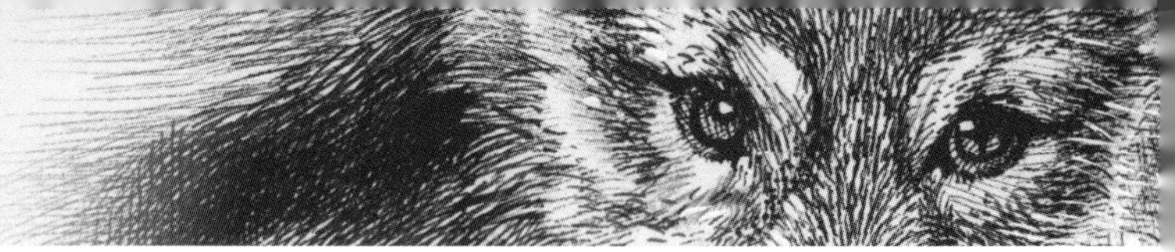

Curricula correlation

English National Curriculum

Spoken language	Articulate and justify answers, arguments and opinions
Word reading	Apply knowledge of root words and suffixes (etymology and morphology) to understand the meaning of new words they meet
Comprehension	Infer characters' feelings, thoughts and motives from their actions and justify inferences with detailed evidence
	Discuss words and phrases that capture the reader's interest and imagination
	Participate in discussion about books, taking turns and listening to what others say

Developing grammar, punctuation, vocabulary and spelling

Grammar and Punctuation	Use of adverbs	usually, carefully, easily, quietly, prickly, fully, eagerly, safely, suddenly, pitifully, finally, mournfully, freely, frantically, unfriendly, instantly, joyfully
	Use of the forms *a* or *an* according to whether the next word begins with a consonant or a vowel	An hour, a big stag
Vocabulary and Spelling	The suffix *-ly*	usually, carefully, easily, quietly, prickly, fully, eagerly, safely, suddenly, pitifully, finally, mournfully, freely, frantically, unfriendly, instantly, joyfully
	Challenge and context words	snarl, howl, pounce, hunting, loping, she-wolf, fangs, hooves, antlers, marrow, coat, pack, wilderness, carcass, territory, pack

Reading assessment points

Word reading	Can the children read independently using a range of strategies appropriately, including decoding, to establish meaning?
Comprehension	Can the children identify where language is used to create mood, build tension or paint a picture?
	Can the children empathise with different characters' point of view in order to explain what characters are thinking/feeling and the way they act?
	Can the children discuss reasons for actions and events based on evidence in the text?

Scottish Curriculum for Excellence

Listening and talking	When listening and talking with others, for different purposes, I can exchange information, experiences, explanations, ideas and opinions **LIT 1–09a**
Reading	To show my understanding, I can respond to different kinds of questions and other close reading tasks and I am learning to create some questions of my own **ENG 1–17a**
	I can share my thoughts about structure, characters and/or setting, recognise the writer's message and relate it to my own experiences, and I can comment on the effective choice of words and other features **ENG 1–19a**

Welsh National Literacy Framework

Oracy	Explain information and ideas using relevant vocabulary (Speaking)
Reading	Accurately identify the topic and main ideas of a text, *e.g. by highlighting, using key words of the text* (Comprehension)
	Deduce ideas and information by linking explicit statements, *e.g. cause and effect* (Comprehension)
	Speak clearly, varying expression to help listeners (Speaking)

Northern Ireland Curriculum

Talking and listening	Read aloud from a variety of sources, including their own work, inflecting appropriately to emphasise meaning
Reading	Use a range of comprehension skills, both oral and written, to interpret and discuss texts
	Express opinions and give reasons based on what they have read

Session I (Chapters I–3)

About this book

This story tracks the life of Grey – a wolf cub who is shot and separated from his family pack. Through his difficulties he develops independence and determination that makes him a great leader to a large pack of wolves.

You will need

- *Wolf words* Photocopy Master, *Teaching Handbook* for Year 3/P4
- *Timeline of Grey's awful day* Photocopy Master, *Teaching Handbook* for Year 3/P4

Before reading

- Ask the children what stories they know about wolves, e.g. 'Little Red Riding Hood'. What characteristics does the wolf have in these stories? What facts – if any – do the children know about wolves? **(activating prior knowledge)**
- Do they see any contradiction in the title *Lone Wolf*? What does the title make them think the story might be about? **(predicting)**
- Read the back cover blurb and read the chapter titles. What does the final heading 'Grey's pack' suggest about the ending? **(previewing, predicting)**
- Read the opening page aloud to the group. Then ask them in pairs to read it to each other, using expression. Ask them not to read on to the next page, until told to do so. **(engaging readers and encouraging fluent reading)**

During reading

- Ask the children to reread the opening page again, silently, and then read on to the end of Chapter 3.
- As they read, ask them to notice who is in the wolf pack and what are their different roles.
- Ask the the children to look for words that end with the suffix *-ly* and make a list as they read.
- If you have not already done so, ask the children what to do if they encounter a difficult word, modelling with an example from the book if necessary.

Assessment point

Can the children read independently using a range of strategies appropriately, including decoding, to establish meaning?

After reading

Returning to the text

Ask the children:

- Why has the author started with the shooting incident?
- How does she make us feel sorry for the cub? (By the descriptions and words suggesting Grey's vulnerability.)
- In what ways does the wolf pack defend their cubs?
- What features of the wolves physical characteristics help it to defend itself?
- How did Grey get separated from his family? Was it his own fault? **(deducing, inferring, drawing conclusions)**

Assessment point
Can the children identify where language is used to create mood, build tension or paint a picture?

Developing comprehension

- Begin filling in the *Timeline of Grey's awful day* Photocopy Master. **(summarizing)**
- Ask the children to describe how Grey must feel being away from his family. How do they think his close family members, especially Grandma, must be feeling? **(empathizing)**

Assessment point
Can the children sometimes empathise with different characters' point of view in order to explain what characters are thinking/feeling and the way they act?

Developing grammar, punctuation and spelling

- Look at the list of words that the children have made. Explain that these are adverbs (words that give more information about a verb, adjective or another adverb). Discuss the spelling of the words ending *-ly*. How does the root word sometimes change before the *-ly* is added? (If the verb ends in a 'y', remove the 'y', add an 'i' and then add -ly.)

Developing fluency

- Record the chapter describing Grey's adventure in the river. Add the sound effects of water and wolves howling. **(visualizing and other sensory responses)**

Session 2 (Chapters 4 and 5)

Before reading

- Ask the children to recap what has happened in the story so far. **(activating prior knowledge)**
- Can they deduce by the headings what the next two chapters will be about? **(predicting, deducing, inferring, drawing conclusions)**
- You may wish to practise decoding some of the challenge and context words. **(introducing new vocabulary)**

During reading

- Ask the children to read Chapters 4 and 5.
- As they read, ask them to think about what things go well and what things go badly for Grey.

After reading

Returning to the text

Ask the children:

- How did the family try to get Grey back?
- Why did Grey's mum keep howling?
- What things went badly and what things went well for Grey in these chapters?
- Do they think Grey will survive? **(deducing, inferring, drawing conclusions)**

Developing comprehension

- Ask the children to describe some of the incidents in these two chapters from Grey's viewpoint. **(empathizing, deducing, inferring, drawing conclusions)**

Assessment point

Can the children discuss reasons for actions and events based on evidence in the text?

Developing grammar, punctuation and spelling

- Point out the determiner in the sentence *An hour passed, maybe more.* (p.27). Now compare it to the determiner in the sentence But a big stag turned towards him ... (p.32). Explain that both *a* and *an* are used to mean a single thing. You use *an* if the noun following it starts with a vowel.

Session 3 (Chapters 6–8)

Before reading

- Ask the children to recap what has happened in the story so far. **(activating prior knowledge)**
- Look at the last three chapter headings. How do they think Grey's life is turning around? **(predicting, deducing, inferring, drawing conclusions)**

During reading

- Ask the children to read Chapters 6–8.
- As they read, ask them to notice how the author portrays Grey in these chapters.

After reading

Returning to the text

Ask the children:

- Why does Grey quiver with excitement on page 36?
- Why did Grey and the other wolf fight when Grey approached the pack?
- Why do you think the attacking pack spread out when they were about to attack Grey's pack?
- How did the wolves recognize each other as family? (By sound and smell.)
- What image of Grey is created in Chapter 8? How does the author do this?

Developing comprehension

- Create a timeline for Grey's life, outlining Grey's life from birth to becoming the leader of the large pack.

Developing vocabulary

- Search for and list all the words that describe the settings. What impression of the countryside do these give?
- List words to describe the noises Grey makes. Sort these into categories, e.g. noises when he is feeling frightened or alone; noises when he is feeling at ease/in a pack. What effect do these words have on the reader?

Assessment point
Can the children identify where language is used to create mood, build tension or paint a picture?

Follow-up

Writing activities

- Discuss the children's overall impressions of the book. Invite them to write a book review for this story. **(longer writing task)**
- Make a comic strip or graphic novel version of the incident with the hunter or another dramatic incident in the story, using speech and thought bubbles and captions to tell the story. **(short writing task)**
- Using the book and other sources, write a non-information report on wild wolves and their lives. **(longer writing task)**

Other literacy activities

- Ask the children to imagine they are a hunter and to justify to a partner their decision to shoot a young wolf. **(spoken language)**
- List words describing a wolf's physical appearance. Write these around the picture on the *Wolf words* Photocopy Master.

Cross-curricular activities

- Research and locate on a map places where wolves still live in the wild. **(Geography)**
- Turn the information report on wolves into a software presentation and encourage the children to deliver this to other classes. **(Computing)**
- Consider the arguments for and against hunting. **(PSHE)**
- Listen to a recording of *Peter and the Wolf* and/or watch a film of the story. **(Music)**

Under Attack!

BY MICK GOWAR

Curricula correlation

English National Curriculum

Spoken language	Use relevant strategies to build their vocabulary
Word reading	Apply knowledge of root words and suffixes (etymology and morphology) to understand the meaning of new words they meet
Comprehension	Identify main ideas drawn from more than one paragraph and summarise these
	Retrieve and record information from non-fiction
	Check the text makes sense, discussing understanding and explaining the meaning of words in context

Developing grammar, punctuation, vocabulary and spelling

Grammar and Punctuation	Formation of nouns using suffix *-er*	invader, defender
Vocabulary and Spelling	Endings which sound like /shun/, spelt *-tion*	protection, ammunition, positions, stations, motion, precautions
	Word families based on common words	invader, attacker, defender
	Challenge and context words	security, alarm, invaders, drawbridge, fortified, enemy, soldiers, ramparts, siege, keep, trebuchet, mangonel, archer, notorious, fought, samurai, bastions, Transylvania, medieval

Reading assessment points

Word reading	Can the children read independently using a range of strategies appropriately, including decoding, to establish meaning?
Comprehension	Can the children explore potential meanings of ambitious vocabulary read in context, using knowledge of etymology (*the word origin*), morphology (*the form and structure of a word, i.e. the 'root' word plus prefix and/or suffix*), or the context of the word?
	Can the children summarise and explain the main points in a text, referring back to the text to support this?
	Are the children able to quote directly from the text to support thoughts and discussions?

Scottish Curriculum for Excellence

Listening and talking objectives	As I listen or watch, I can identify and discuss the purpose, key words and main ideas of the text, and use this information for a specific purpose LIT 1-04a
Reading objectives	I can share my thoughts about the structure, characters and/or setting ENG 1-19a
	I can use my knowledge of sight vocabulary, phonics context clues, punctuation and grammar to read with understanding and expression ENG 1-12a
	Using what I know about the features of different types of texts, I can find, select, sort and use information for a specific purpose LIT 1-14a

Welsh National Literacy Framework

Oracy	Organise what they say so that listeners can understand, *e.g. emphasising key points, sequencing an explanation* (Speaking)
Reading	Use a range of strategies to make meaning from words and sentences, including knowledge of phonics, word roots, word families, syntax, text organisation and prior knowledge of context (Reading strategies)
	Accurately identify the topic and main ideas of a text, *e.g. by highlighting, using key words of the text* (Comprehension)

Northern Ireland Curriculum

Talking and Listening	Express thoughts, feelings and opinions in response to personal experiences, imaginary situations, literature, media and curricular topics and activities
Reading	Read, explore, understand and make use of a range of traditional and digital texts

Session 1 (pages 2–9)

About this book

This non-fiction text explains different methods used for defence: water, walls, weapons, alarms and security cameras. It also features impressive examples of defences from around the world, such as famous castles and walls.

You will need

- *Note-taking frame* Photocopy Master, *Teaching Handbook* for Year 3/P4

Before reading

- Look at the front cover and title. Ask the children how they think this book will fit into the theme of strong defences. **(predicting)**
- Ask them to recall any castles they have visited or seen on film. What defensive features did they have? **(activating prior knowledge)**
- Look at the contents page. Ask the children to identify the five different categories of defensive features the book describes. Categorize them into ones which were used hundreds of years ago and ones which are more modern. **(previewing)**

During reading

- Ask the children to read to the end of page 9.
- As they read, ask them to notice the different ways water is used as a defensive feature.
- If you have not already done so, ask the children what to do if they encounter a difficult word, modelling with an example from the book if necessary. «««

Assessment point

Can the children read independently using a range of strategies appropriately, including decoding, to establish meaning?

After reading

Returning to the text

Ask the children to:

- give some reasons why water is a good form of defence
- explain how people got across the moats
- give some examples of castles where the sea was used as a defence. **(recall)**

Developing comprehension

- Ask the children to use the photograph on page 8 to draw a bird's eye view of the castle and its moat. **(visualizing)**
- Allow the children time to make notes on the *Note-taking frame* Photocopy Master on the pages read during this session. **(determining importance, summarizing)**

Developing vocabulary

- Record words that relate to attacking, defending, people who live or work in castles, and weapons.

Developing grammar, punctuation and spelling

- Ask the children to highlight the nouns in their vocabulary lists, e.g. *invader*, *defender*. What do these words have in common? Draw attention to the fact that they are nouns made by adding the suffix *-er* to a verb. Can they think of any more? Can they find an example that doesn't fit this rule? (archer)
- Look at and discuss the core words *invade* and *defend*. Demonstrate how suffixes can be added to form new words. Form word families for the core words *invade* (*invaders, invasive, invasion, invading*) and *defend* (*defenders, defensive, defences, defending*).

Assessment point

Can the children explore potential meanings of ambitious vocabulary read in context, using knowledge of etymology (*the word origin*), morphology (*the form and structure of a word, i.e. the 'root' word plus prefix and/or suffix*), or the context of the word?

Session 2 (pages 10–15)

Before reading

- Ask the children to recap what they learnt about water defences. **(recall, summarizing)**
- Look at the next heading in the contents page: 'Walls'. Can the children predict how walls could be a good form of defence? **(previewing, predicting, deducing, inferring)**

- You may wish to practise decoding some of the challenge and context words.

During reading

- Ask the children to read pages 10–15.
- As they read, ask them to notice the different types of walls used for defence.

After reading

Returning to the text

Ask the children to:

- give reasons why walls are a good form of defence
- give some examples of castles built on cliffs or hills. Why are these difficult to attack? Encourage them to draw information from the illustrations as well as the text.
- Why do they think sloping walls were used for some castles? **(recall, deducing, inferring, drawing conclusions)**

Assessment point
Can the children summarise and explain the main points in a text, referring back to the text to support this?

Developing comprehension

- Allow children time to make notes on the *Note-taking frame* Photocopy Master on the pages read during this session. **(determining importance, summarizing)**

- Before Session 3, ask the children to read pages 16–21 independently.

Session 3 (pages 22–30)

Before reading

- Ask the children to recap what kind of ammunition and defences were used during a siege or attack. **(recall, summarizing)**
- Invite the children to explain why an arrow slit was used by an archer, synthesizing the information from both the text and illustrations on pages 10 and 20. **(synthesizing)**

- Check the children's understanding and pronunciation of the names of the weapons – *trebuchet* (p.18) and *mangonel* (p.19) and other defence/attack words such as *ammunition* (p.18).
- Ask the children to explain how they worked out the meanings of these words by using the context. **(introducing new vocabulary)**

Assessment point
Can the children explore potential meanings of ambitious vocabulary read in context, using knowledge of etymology (*the word origin*), morphology (*the form and structure of a word, i.e. the 'root' word plus prefix and/or suffix*), or the context of the word?

During reading

- Ask the children to read pages 22–30.
- As they read, ask them to decide whether they are for or against security cameras based on the points in the text.
- As they read, ask them to make a note of words ending *-tion*.

After reading

Returning to the text

- Ask the children why alarms protect people. Why are closed circuit alarms placed by doors and windows? Why do alarms often make a lot of noise? **(recall, deducing, inferring, drawing conclusions)**

Developing comprehension

- Allocate to each child one reason for or against security cameras. Ask them to come up with an example or evidence to support their point. Hold a class debate on the issue. **(synthesizing)**
- Allow children time to make notes on the *Note-taking frame* Photocopy Master. **(determining importance, summarizing)**

Assessment point
Are the children able to quote directly from the text to support thoughts and discussions?

Developing grammar, punctuation and spelling

- Draw attention to some words the children have found ending with *-tion*, e.g. *protection*, *station*. Ask the children to read these. What sound does this ending make? (/shun/) Do they know any other ways of spelling this sound? (*-sion*, *-ssion*, *-cian*)

Follow-up

Writing activities

- Reread the nursery rhyme 'Humpty Dumpty' on page 21. Consider its rhythm and simple rhyme structure. Write a rhyme about one of the attacks by the X-bots. Children could use one of these starting lines or invent their own: *Twenty X-bots crossing a pond .../A fleet of X-bots high in the sky ...* **(short writing task)**
- Design warning signs for guard dogs and other animal guards. **(short writing task)**
- Write an imaginary account of a siege using siege weaponry and machinery from the point of view of an attacker or a defender. **(longer writing task)**

Other literacy activities

- Using the notes made on the *Note-taking frame* Photocopy Master, ask the children to prepare a brief talk on strong defences. They could make an audio recording of the report. **(spoken language, presentation)**

Cross-curricular activities

- Visit a local castle and look at its defensive features. **(History)**
- Build a model castle with several defensive features. **(DT)**
- Experiment to see why curved walls are stronger than walls with right angles. **(Science, DT)**
- Make a freeze frame animation of a castle attack using the model castle and small world figures. Record a sound track for the film. **(Computing, Music)**
- Play a game of football, netball or another attacking/defending game. Video the game. Watch it to identify and analyze points where the defence was particularly strong or particularly weak and identify why. **(PE)**

Strong Defences

BY HAYDN MIDDLETON

Curricula correlation

English National Curriculum

Spoken language	Articulate and justify answers, arguments and opinions
Word reading	Apply knowledge of root words and prefixes (etymology and morphology), to understand the meaning of new words they meet
Comprehension	Read books that are structured in different ways and for a range of purposes
	Use dictionaries to check the meaning of words that they have read
	Listen to and discuss a range of non-fiction and reference books

Developing grammar, punctuation, vocabulary and spelling

Grammar and Punctuation	How the prefix *un-* changes the meaning of adjectives	unwell, unfriendly, untrue
Vocabulary and Spelling	Word families based on common words	vaccines, vaccinated, vaccination immune, immunity
	Challenge and context words	viruses, antibodies, immunity, vaccines, bacteria, blood, polio, vaccinated, measles, mumps, parasites, territories, Bangladesh, Martians, extraterrestrials, satellites, security, antibiotics, siege, military

Reading assessment points

Word reading	Can the children read independently using a range of strategies appropriately, including decoding, to establish meaning?
Comprehension	Can the children understand the purpose of a paragraph/chapter *(the way in which writers use paragraphs and chapters to group related ideas together)?*
	Are the children able to quote directly from the text to support thoughts and discussions?

Scottish Curriculum for Excellence

Listening and talking objectives	I can select ideas and relevant information, organize these in a logical sequence and use words which will be interesting and/or useful for others LIT 1-06a
Reading objectives	I can use my knowledge of sight vocabulary, phonics, context clues, punctuation and grammar to read with understanding and expression ENG 1-12a
	To show my understanding across different areas of learning, I can identify and consider the purpose and main ideas of a text LIT 1-16a

Welsh National Literacy Framework

Oracy	Explain information and ideas using relevant vocabulary (Speaking)
Reading	Identify how texts are organised, *e.g. lists, numbered points, diagrams with arrows, tables and bullet points* (Reading strategies)
	Use information from texts in their discussions or writing

Northern Ireland Curriculum

Talking and Listening	Express thoughts, feelings and opinions in response to personal experiences, imaginary situations, literature, media and curricular topics and activities
Reading	Begin to use evidence from text to support their views
	Explore and begin to understand how texts are structured in a range of genres

Session 1 (pages 2–9)

This non-fiction book uses both formal and informal report styles to explore strong defences adopted by humans and animals.

You will need

- *Vocabulary detectives* Photocopy Master, *Teaching Handbook* for Year 3/P4

Before reading

- Ask the children what they know about how animals and humans defend themselves. **(activating prior knowledge)**
- Read page 2 together. Discuss whether the bullet point list outlines the structure and content of the book. Compare this list to the contents page. Do they cover the same topics? Why has author has structured this page in this way? **(previewing)**
- Ask someone in the group to read the page written by the doctor (p.3). Then ask the children to explain what they think the three ways mean before telling them to read on independently. **(engaging readers, encouraging fluent reading)**

During reading

- Ask the children to read to the end of page 9.
- As they read, ask them to look out for scientific words such as *virus*, *vaccination*, *temperature* and *energy*.
- If you have not already done so, ask the children what to do if they encounter a difficult word, modelling with an example from the book if necessary.

Assessment point

Can the children read independently using a range of strategies appropriately, including decoding, to establish meaning?

After reading

Returning to the text

Ask the children:

- What are the three ways your body can fight viruses?
- What can combat bacteria?
- Can they give two examples of how plants and animals save energy?

Developing comprehension

- Ask the children to summarize the information on these pages into three or four main points for each topic covered. **(summarizing, determining importance)**
- Encourage the children to debate the claim 'attack is the best form of defence'. **(adopting a critical stance, debating)**

Developing vocabulary

- Create lists of scientific words as the children read, using the *Vocabulary detectives* Photocopy Master.

Developing grammar, punctuation and spelling

- Look at the scientific words that the children have found. Focus on the core words *vaccine* (noun) and *immune* (adjective). Look for similar words, e.g. *vaccinated* (verb), *vaccination* (noun), *immunity* (noun). Look at how the words are formed. Do children know the verb form of *immune*? (*Immunize*.) Encourage the children to use dictionaries to add to the word groups and sort them into topic-based word families, e.g. based around 'illness' or 'vaccination'.

Session 2 (pages 10–19)

Before reading

- Ask the children to describe as many examples of defence that they have read about so far. Compare these with the features listed in Session 1. **(activating prior knowledge)**
- Glance through pages 10–19. What topics are being discussed? **(previewing)**

During reading

- Ask the children to read pages 10–19.
- As they read, ask them to look at the ways the information is presented.
- Ask the children to look out for words containing the prefix *un-* as they read through.

After reading

Returning to the text

Ask the children:

- How is the Martian report on pages 10–13 organized? (Chronologically, gives a description with an example.)
- What are the organizational and language features of the catalogue? (pp.14–15)
- How does the naturalist's report (pp.16–19) differ from the formal Martian's report?

Assessment point

Can the children understand the purpose of a paragraph/chapter *(the way in which writers use paragraphs and chapters to group related ideas together)*?

Developing comprehension

- Create a grid comparing the defensive features of castles and gated communities. Additional information can be taken from *Under Attack!* **(synthesizing)**

Developing grammar, punctuation and spelling

- Ask the children to look at the examples they've found of the prefix *un-*, e.g *unwell*, *unfriendly*. Can they determine its meaning (not) from the context of the word? Can they think of any other similar words? Can *un-* be added to every word or are there exceptions, e.g. *nice*?

Developing fluency

- Allow the children, in pairs, to read the advertisements of defensive devices (pp.14–15) to each other in the style of television advertising.

Session 3 (pages 20–30)

Before reading

- Ask the children to summarize the defences they have read so far that animals use. **(activating prior knowledge)**
- Read the heading on page 20. What does *Protecting your patch* mean? **(previewing)**

During reading

- Ask the children to read pages 20–30.
- As they read, ask them to think about how satellites are a type of defence for the planet.

After reading

Returning to the text

Ask the children:

- How do structures protect territory from attack and from water?
- How do robins protect their territory?
- How do satellites protect us?

Assessment point

Are the children able to quote directly from the text to support thoughts and discussions?

Developing fluency

- Listen to a clip from a radio naturalist programme on the BBC website. Note the presentational features. Encourage children to role-play being a naturalist broadcaster with pages from this book as the script.

Follow-up

Writing activities

- Children could write a descriptive account from their own experience of what it feels like to have a cold. **(short writing task)**
- Look at pages 14–15. Also, look at other examples of sales catalogues. Note the features: image, brief description, price. Make a catalogue of siege machines. **(short writing task)**
- Write a Martian report on defensive/attacking games such as football or netball. **(longer writing task)**

Other literacy activities

- Once the children have read all of the books in the cluster, orally review them and ask the children to say which is their favourite and why. **(spoken language, discussion)**

Cross-curricular activities

- Research one of the animals in the book to find out what nutrition they need and where they get this from. **(Science)**
- Using a computer, to create an electronic catalogue of protective clothing used in skateboarding, biking and motor racing. **(Computing)**
- Research smoke alarms and design an advertising poster to persuade people to have one in their homes. **(PSHE, Art and Design, DT)**